I0814462

How do we understand what was, grapple with what is and prepare for what is likely to be, as a nation, as a people, as a community, as individuals?

This series is an attempt to address this question by putting into print thoughts, ideas and concerns of some of South Asia's most seminal thinkers.

In memory of Kozo Yamamura (1934–2017)

HISTORY FOR PEACE TRACTS

JERRY PINTO
Thinking Aloud

SOHAIL HASHMI
The Music of Stones

JANAKI NAIR
Is a Single Teachable Indian Past Possible Today?

GAYATRI CHAKRAVORTY SPIVAK
AND ROMILA THAPAR
The Idea of India

DEEPA SREENIVAS
Remaking the Citizen for New Times

KRISHNA KUMAR
Learning to Live with the Past

YOUSUF SAEED
Partitioning Bazaar Art

RAJEEV BHARGAVA
Reimagining Indian Secularism

Looking Back through Our Identities

Itihāsa-Purāṇa

ALOKA PARASHER SEN

LONDON NEW YORK CALCUTTA

The text in this volume is an updated edition of a lecture delivered for History for Peace in 2020.

Visit historyforpeace.pw to read similar resources.

All images reproduced in this book have been taken from Wikimedia Commons and are in the public domain.

Seagull Books, 2025

First published in volume form
by Seagull Books, 2025

ISBN 978 1 80309 479 3

British Library Cataloguing-in-Publication Data

A catalogue record for this book
is available from the British Library

Typeset by Seagull Books, Calcutta, India

Printed and bound by WordsWorth India,
New Delhi, India

LAKṢMĪ NARASIṀHA TEMPLE, AHOBILAM

‘[O]ne day the Hindu god Narsima fell in love with one of the most beautiful Chenchu girls. The beautiful Chenchu girl was called Chenchistral, but even though the god Narsima took her to his home and called her Chenchi Lachmi and she lived with the god’s own wife, who was called Ardi [*sic*] Lachmi, she was very unhappy. And she prayed that in future all Chenchu girls should be born ugly with crooked noses and ugly eyes and black skin, for if they were born beautiful, the Nawabs and the Sahibs and even the gods would come and take them away.’[1]

This is a well-entrenched myth among the Chenchus, an autochthonous Adivasi group living along the Nallamala Hills in Andhra Pradesh. In the ethnologist Christoph von Fürer-Haimendorf's telling of it, there seems to be a very thin line between myth and history as we know it: the gods are put on the same pedestal as nawabs and sahibs. Von Fürer-Haimendorf mainly conducted his fieldwork in the early 1940s in the former princely state of Hyderabad, where the Chenchus must have been in contact with the elite groups of the region.

In the late nineteenth century, Edgar Thurston, drawing on the work of the medieval historian Firishta, wrote:

> [The] Chenchus are described [by Firishta] as 'exceedingly black, with

> long hair, and on their heads wore caps made of the leaves of trees. Each man had with him unbarbed arrows and a bow for hunting. They molest no one and live in caverns or under the shady branches of trees.'[2]

In Firishta's account, there is no reference to the 'Chenchi Lachmi' myth, but when Thurston turns to the Madras Census Report of 1891, he informs us of another tribe called the Yanadis. There is some confusion, Thurston reports, about whether the Chenchus are distinct from the Yanadis, Bonthuk Savaras, Irulas and other tribes who live in the same area, or whether they are one and the same and are simply known by different names throughout the geography. Like the

Chenchus, the Yanadis are said 'to worship a god called Chenchu Devata' and the Bonthuk Savaras are said to believe in the myth of the Chenchu girl being carried away by Narasiṃha.[3] The image seems to be deeply embedded in the collective memory of the Chenchu people for generations. And it compels us to reflect on the contemporary reality of Chenchu women being exploited for their bodies.

Thurston also draws our attention to the fact that many of the Chenchus regard Narasiṃha, whom they call Obalesudu, as their brother-in-law and continue to 'go to the temple for the annual festival [and] carry cloths as presents for the god and goddess'.[4] Today, Narasiṃha is firmly entrenched as the family deity of a section of the Chenchu people, who thereby enjoy certain privileges in the temples of Ahobilam, famous for its nine Narasiṃha shrines.

We shall return to this story and this myth later, but with yet another myth, that is, the myth of the outsiders narrating how this happened. The critic Ashis Nandy once wrote,

> [M]illions of people still live outside 'history'. They do have theories of the past; they do believe that the past is important and shapes the present and the future, but they also recognize, confront and live with a past different from that constructed by historians and historical consciousness. They even have a different way of arriving at that past.[5]

But what do we mean by history? And by myth? Terms such as these bear a certain genealogy, and if thoughtlessly applied to all social situations, they can have disastrous effects. Rather than looking for a pristine purity within each of these terms, one must explore how the human mind tries to construct them in various phases throughout history.

The Oxford English Dictionary defines myth as 'a traditional story, especially one concerning the early history of a people or explaining a natural or social phenomenon, intimately involving supernatural beings or events.' Usually, this is an unapproved or false collective belief that is used to justify a social institution. Myths give us an account of gods and superhuman beings, but they refer to a time that is unspecified and, therefore, very difficult to place in ordinary human chronology. Returning to its Greco-Roman roots, mythos is usually seen in binary opposition to logos.

The terms *logos* and *mythos* represent two different approaches to understanding the world. Truth discovered through logos seeks to be objective and universal, relying on explanations, observable facts, controlled experiments and deductive proofs. In contrast, truth derived from myth, of course, is considered more subjective, rooted in individual feelings and experiences.

Modern history, as a discipline, distinguishes itself from the more traditional modes of looking at the past by claiming objectivity, which is seen as a mark of superiority. It relies on concrete evidence, which supposedly results in certitude in historical narratives. As a result, this mode of historical inquiry has become the dominant mode of constructing the past across much of the world. To quote Ashis Nandy, the dominance of history is linked to 'the modern nation-state, the secular worldview, the Baconian concept of scientific rationality, nineteenth-century theories of progress, and, in recent decades, development.'[6]

When this historical mode was imposed on the colonized world, it selectively invented their collective pasts. Once independent, these societies used history to celebrate official and national regenerations, selectively glorifying great events. This was particularly prominent in those countries gripped by national movements, where these exaggerated notions of the self were forged by selectively drawing upon the past. At the same time, this also tended to absolutize the past, affecting cultures that had lived with open-ended concepts of history, depending on myths, legends and epics to define their cultural selves. This can be observed in societies across Africa, South America and Asia. It also helped to calcify civilizational, cultural and national boundaries. The power of the new ideology—by which I mean history, a certain way of looking at the past—enhanced the power of the discipline, because there was no viable critique from within the discipline itself. Indeed, as Dipesh Chakrabarty argued, the muse of Indian history remains caught in an impossible situation, being able only to mimic 'a certain "modern" subject of "European" history and is bound to represent a sad figure of lack and failure.'[7]

Those who lived outside history were, in a sense, ahistorical, without a proper historical consciousness as delineated by the European Enlightenment. The only option available was to bring these 'ahistoricals' into history. Naturally, those whose understanding of the past differed from this model were relegated to the realm of the irrational. The Orientalist constructions of the 'other' are a case in point.

A myth, then, as we understand it in the modern context, is primarily understood as a story based on imagination and continual retelling, making it antithetical to history in its modern incarnation, and history has thus looked down on myth.

It is very difficult to find precise equivalents for the terms *myth* and *history* in Sanskrit and other Indian languages.

In Hindi, for instance, danta kathā, literally folk legends or folklore, refers to stories about mythical or supernatural beings or events, which may be local or migratory. L. P. Vidyarthi, D. N. Bhagvat and other scholars have clarified the various terms, definitions, propositions and concepts in the study of folklore in India and have suggested that the synonym of myth in Hindi should be daivata kathā and not purān kathā. The latter is usually associated with a popular class of Hindu literature known as the Purāṇas, which fall in the category of dharma kathā, literally 'moral tales'. The scholar Śaunaka, well known as the commentator of the Vedas, uses the term pavitra kathā (sacred tales) 'since myths are associated with sacred themes'.[8] Thus, we may conclude that danta kathās were folktales that became popular over generations and were often recited as songs or poems. These stories were purely imaginary, lacking any tangible basis in reality, yet they had been passed down from time immemorial. However, they were distinct from the kalpita kathās, which in Hindi refers to fables designed to impart moral teachings.

Kalpita kathās are products of a highly developed literary genius, and though not found in the Vedas, they are well known in the Mahābhārata and Jātaka tradition of storytelling. It is important to note that animals serve as powerful symbols in these kathās.

A wide variety of kathās are found in different regional contexts; the well-known sādhu kathās of Assam were, for instance, stories narrated by wandering mendicants.

While the term *kathā* refers to a type of story, and the Hindi word *mithaka*, a distant descendant of the Greek *mythos*, may encompass the idea of myth, a closer equivalent would be the terms *purāṇik* or *purāṇa*, that refer to something ancient.

This differs from the Purāṇas, a distinct class of texts that not only explore myths and legends but also contain information on the geography of the subcontinent, genealogies of ruling dynasties in North India and the various sectarian traditions within Hinduism.

How, then, should we understand the term Itihāsa-Purāṇa? I don't want to treat these two words simplistically, as binary opposites. Conventionally, but incorrectly, they are understood as narrations of events as they happened in the past. Some interpretations differentiate purāṇa from itihāsa, suggesting that the latter refers to incidents narrated during the lifetime of the storyteller, leading to the assertion that itihāsa represents 'what actually happened'.

This view equates itihāsa with history as we understand it today, despite relying on texts embedded in a vastly different worldview that were initially transmitted in oral form.

I want to suggest a more nuanced understanding of these terms, avoiding their separation into distinct entities. In ancient literature, purāṇa is frequently linked with itihāsa, forming the composite term Itihāsa-Purāṇa. This expression appears in the Vedas—specifically the Atharva and Rig Vedas—though without emphasis. It is in the Upaniṣads that they are collectively referred to as the fifth Veda.

The term *purāṇa* literally means 'ancient' or 'of antiquity'. A typical Purāṇa begins with a creation myth, followed by accounts of humanity's emergence, genealogies of major ruling dynasties and narratives set in the Kali Yuga (the age of Kali, or the age of vice and misery). These stories often feature gods intervening in human affairs, caught up in a search for the meaning of life, grappling with moral dilemmas, good and evil, right and wrong. These trials and tribulations are what make them gods and define their divinity. Such stories thus weave the cosmic with the divine and the human. The godhead is not a distant dictator of human affairs but is living through life with all its horrors and joys.

The term *itihāsa* literally means 'thus it was' (iti ha āsa) or 'so it has been', referring to accounts of the past. It generally encompasses the epics—the Mahābhārata and the Rāmāyaṇa—and writings on subjects such as cosmogony, creation, genealogies, geography, time, sectarian beliefs, rituals, pilgrimages and more.

Thus, linking itihāsa with purāṇa suggests that history and mythology are inseparable. But within ancient Indian philosophical traditions, itihāsa and purāṇa do not occupy a very high epistemological status because they are based on memory. Memory is considered unreliable—it does not generate new knowledge and depends on recollection for authentication. As such, these texts loosely represent the historical consciousness of a society: what it chooses to remember as significant for its identity. This remembered history spans personal recollections of the living to the civilizational ideals embedded in scriptures and the classics.

In his studies on the Middle East, Bernard Lewis describes this phenomenon as a society's 'inherited historiography' or 'the collective memory of a community or nation or other entity—what it, or its rulers and leaders, poets and sages, choose to remember as significant, both as reality and symbol.'[9] Similarly, Itihāsa-Purāṇa does not refer to precise accounts of what happened in the past, since it encompasses the intermingling of different forms of memory, as well as a connotation of a timeless history. It does not claim to recount the exact historical truth, but instead grapples with the legacy of an inherited paramparā, loosely translated as tradition, that balances continuity with fluidity.

There are other terms in the ancient Indian tradition that refer to the past: gātha, carita, ākhyāyana, vamsa and more. But none explicitly denote a sequential chronicling of events.

Against this backdrop, it is challenging for modern historians to apply the tools of the scientific method to unravel the truths within myths, because these narratives were never meant to serve as evidence for historical events. Yet it is essential to engage with them—not only because embedded within them are questions of the philosophy of life, but also because they embody the multiple identities of our past.

Romila Thapar's *The Past Before Us* differentiates between various traditions of understanding historical time in early North India and examines how Sanskrit and Pali terms reflected these perspectives. She identifies phases where history was initially embedded in Vedic traditions, the Mahābhārata and the Rāmāyaṇa. This was followed by its emergence in the vaṁśānucarita (genealogies of royal dynasties) sections of the Purāṇas, and later externalized in biographies framed as histories within the Brahmanical tradition. Thapar contrasts these with alternative histories found in Buddhist and Jain texts. Her analysis emphasizes a plurality of traditions and a multiplicity of voices, each articulating unique ways of perceiving, remembering and documenting the past.

Thapar highlights the Viṣṇu Purāṇa as an exemplary text within the Itihāsa-Purāṇa tradition, due to its relatively fewer interpolations and cohesive structure. She notes that its composition adheres closely to the five aṁśas (parts) required in a Purāṇa: 'A description of the creation of the world, as well as the geography of the universe, precedes the genealogical section thus providing both a temporal and spatial context to the past. It also provides a context to the eschatology of the Purāṇas.'[10]

She writes: 'Interspersing genealogies with legends and myths created a transition between myth and that past which was perceived to have happened.'[11] The section on geography (pratisarga) focuses on cosmic and earthly dimensions, centring Jambudvīpa as the heart of the world. The third aṁśa delves into cosmological time—the kalpa, manvantara and yugas—and explores how Viṣṇu embodies time since time too is a creator, preserver and destroyer of the universe. The fourth aṁśa contains the descent lists of the ruling Kṣatriya families in the vaṁśānucarita. She writes:

> [I]ts construction appears to have been based on three sequential periods with distinctly different patterns. The first narrates the period of the Manus narrating myths of creation and cosmology. This period is set aside because of the great Flood, subsequent to which comes the second period. This constructs a record of what

was perceived as the lineages of ruling clans. It traces the descent of the Kṣatriya lineages from their progenitor Manu, via the two main descent groups, the Sūryavaṃśa [Solar dynasty] and the Candravaṃśa [Lunar dynasty]. These include, among others, the families and clans of the Mahābhārata and the Rāmāyaṇa. The third section is a listing of kings and dynasties, reflecting the establishment of kingship and the state. It focuses initially on Magadha and continues up to the Gupta rulers of the mid-first millennium AD, and possibly a little later.

The fifth section recounts Kṛṣṇa's incarnation as Viṣṇu, while the sixth addresses theories of cyclical ages (yugas) and ultimate cosmic destruction: 'Thus the text itself completes the cycle and the reader can return to the beginning with the description of primary creation.'[12]

Thapar analyses how genealogies—whether actual or invented—became central to perceptions of the past. She asks why these genealogies were embedded in texts with religious or sectarian identities. A key feature is their gradual shift towards linear time, reflecting the political identities of the ruling elite. She notes that texts like the Viṣṇu Purāṇa rhetorically question what became of ancient heroes like Rāma or Yudhiṣṭhira: ' "We do not know where they are now, did they actually live?" [4.24.149]. All present and future rulers are subject to the same fate of being forgotten; unless, as is the assumption here, only inclusion in the vaṃśānucarita can prevent that fate.'[13] A fitting conclusion for a text dedicated to recounting rulers of the past.

Thapar draws our attention to the evolving ideas about the past and their articulation across different genres of texts, emphasizing how the nature of memory or 'history' in each set of texts is shaped by its specific context. Moreover, she argues that despite their differences, these sources collectively reveal a process that legitimizes the present by employing both cyclic and linear notions of time.

Thapar invites us to notice parallels between this process and the craft of modern historical writing, where our present-day perspectives shape how we look back at the past. Have we truly retrieved the essence of understanding the past from a different perspective? Should we prioritize the past itself or our present vantage point? Or should we nurture a dialogue between the two? Defining ancient historical traditions using modern standards leaves our historical subjects in a subordinate relationship with us, while at the same time it risks constructing contemporary narratives based on ancient literature. While this literature highlights the perceptions of the past, we often tend to impose our own meanings onto them.

How do we engage with different literary modes to sift apart narrative as fiction from narrative as history?

Furthermore, by using these texts as sources, we often neglect early Indian epistemological traditions—such as nirukta (etymology) and bhāṣya (commentary)—which encourage ongoing reinterpretation and re-examination.

The Eurocentric frameworks that dominate our epistemological perspectives and historical disciplines limit our ability to move beyond the confines of concepts such as analytical teleology and historicism, especially since the sources we consult are open-ended texts, making it difficult for historians to place them within linear time.

Many regional dynasties in India used genealogies to define their identities, particularly in areas marked by intense competition and rivalry, where their authority was under threat. While they helped establish the distinct identity of the ruling elite, genealogical inscriptions (such as praśastis, that is, eulogies or inscriptions of praise, in particular) also enabled them to develop a historical consciousness. This consciousness reaffirmed their greatness by linking them to ancient civilizational symbols and lineages, such as the legendary families of the Sūryavaṁśa (solar dynasty) and the Candravaṁśa (lunar dynasty).

Aruna Pariti's research on the Chalukyan families of the Deccan illustrates how these dynasties prefaced their actual historical genealogies with mythical, legendary or semi-historical ones, drawing from the Itihāsa-Purāṇa tradition.[14] They drew on their gotra (lineage or clan) and kula (family or community) to trace their descent, in their efforts to ground their identities in antiquity. However, these fabricated, mythical genealogies were far removed from their local origins. The semi-historical ones linked them to documented genealogical traditions and vaṁśānucarita sections listing Kali Yuga dynasties as mentioned in the Purāṇas. Historical genealogies, on the other hand, detailed the lineage of past rulers as recounted by the king sanctioning the praśasti, that is, his father, grandfather, great-grandfather and so on.

These genealogies often trace back to both the Sūryavaṁśa and Candravaṁśa. The former is linked to the Ikṣvākus, tracing a direct descent from Aditi and Sūrya, as elaborated in the Rāmāyaṇa. The Candravaṁśa lineage, on the other hand, originates from Ilā, the daughter of Manu—an ambiguous figure with an androgynous identity (Ilā-Ila, both male and female, due to a curse by Śiva)—who married Budha, the son of the moon deity,

Soma. The Mahābhārata expands on this genealogy, referring to it as the Ailā lineage.

Interestingly, many regional and local dynasties in the Deccan adopted this lineage as part of their mythical and legendary past, possibly reflecting their matrilineal traditions. The prominence of matrilineal heritage in this region is evident in the inscriptions of the Sātavāhanas, whose rule preceded that of the Chāḷukyas. Sātavāhana rulers integrated their names with those of their mothers—for instance, Gautamīputra Śātakarṇi and Vasiṣṭhiputra Pulumāvi. The androgynous figure of Ilā, which resonated with their own self-perceptions, is notably referenced in inscriptions of the Chāḷukyas of Veṅgī and Jananāthapuram.[15]

These lineages were not necessarily tied to the geographical origins of ruling families but served to integrate their historical present with a mythical and legendary past. This connection allowed them to assert their identity and dominance over rival elites while reinforcing their understanding of history. As recorded in the Purāṇas, these genealogies became historicized in regions beyond their original context, making it difficult to distinguish myth from history—both of which were crucial in shaping the identity of ruling elites across the subcontinent. Notably, religious affiliation does not appear to have been a significant factor in this process. In this broader context, the Itihāsa-Purāṇa tradition flourished in various regions, each claiming a shared historical consciousness.

How were foreign rulers accommodated or rejected within this view of the past? In the vaṁśānucarita sections, there are brief mentions of foreign ruling elites like the Greeks, Scythians, Pahlavas and Kushanas (referred to as Yavanas, Śakas, Pahlavas and Tusharas respectively in the texts)—rulers of major parts of Northwestern and Northern India during the late centuries BCE and early centuries CE—who are generally categorized as mlecchas, existing outside the varṇa system as Vrātyas or degraded Kṣatriyas. They are thus outside the cultural view of what is the self.

In the Mahābhārata, when the Kṣatriya sage Viśvāmitra was stealing Nandinī, the magical cow of the Brāhmaṇa sage Vasiṣṭha, the cow, from various parts of her body, created an army of these mleccha foreigners in their manifold armours, ready to combat the army of Viśwamitra. Note the contrast: while the four varṇas in the cosmic being mahāpuruṣa have a mythical origin, as far as these foreign groups are concerned, they are born to Nandinī: from her anus, she created the Pahlavas, the Śabaras and the Śakas; from her dung and her urine, she created the Yavanas; and from her foam, she brought forth the Pundras, Kirātas, Dramidas, Simhalas, Barbaras and Daradas.

This mythological construction, though extraordinary, served to reconcile the historical reality of these foreign groups' existence. It offered an explanation for the presence of large armies of foreigners who confronted and likely defeated the existing Kṣatriya elite. The myth of the army's creation interestingly facilitated the Brāhmaṇa's resistance against the Kṣatriya, and this is indicative of how Brāhmaṇas became priests for the newly Brahmanized elites. For instance, inscriptions indicate that the Śakas in Western India granted cows and villages to Brāhmaṇas. These myths thus served two purposes—excluding and incorporating foreign groups at the same time.

The epic traditions of early India have been interpreted in various ways, not solely for their 'historical' content. Scholars recognize that these narratives explore multiple dimensions of the human condition, and their retellings across different historical contexts are layered with complex meanings that cannot be understood in simplistic terms. A closer examination of one such reading reveals:

> The concerns of the Mahābhārata are the concerns of everyday life everywhere. In its inquiry into the human condition it raises those very questions the answers to which we all seek in the diverse circumstances of our lives.[16]

Chaturvedi Badrinath's *The Mahābhārata: An Inquiry in the Human Condition* does not relegate the epic to the distant past; instead, the author presents it as a site where conceptual contradictions, dilemmas, debates and contestations are graphically narrated. These themes, he suggests, are not unique to the epic's protagonists but continue to resonate with our sensibilities across all domains of activity, making the Mahābhārata a text that can be revisited and retold repeatedly.

This perspective is in total opposition to the conventional view of the Mahābhārata as itihāsa. Chaturvedi's interpretation urges us to think of how the contextuality of time and history is necessarily intertwined with ethical issues surrounding the human condition:

> Kāla, 'time', in which everything originates and is destroyed, is not the historical 'time'. Neither is it the 'time' that is physically measured. [. . .] It is the ultimate cause of all happenings. At another level, kāla, 'time', is a measure of appropriateness. It is combined with desha and pātra, 'place' and 'the person concerned' These three desha, kāla and pātra, that is, the 'proper place', the

> 'proper time' and the 'proper person' determine the appropriateness of an act and thus, its meaning. [. . .] At still another level, 'time' as history is examined as giving substance to one's life. The three attributes of history, the 'past', the 'present' and the 'future', and one's relationship with them as one's relationship with one's self, constitutes one of the subjects of the inquiry into the human condition.[17]

Notably, Badrinath highlights that, unlike the Rāmāyaṇa, the Mahābhārata shows minimal narrative variations across its manuscript versions found throughout the subcontinent. This suggests that its retellings and translations focus on a broader discourse about the materiality of life, woven into spiritual terms.

Badrinath expresses several anxieties. First, he critiques the way modern social scientists perceive reality and rely on the scientific method, built on a binary 'either/or' world of polarities. Drawing from the Mahābhārata, he suggests that human life cannot be grasped in fragments; it forms a natural unity and wholeness. Removing any part disrupts the unity, leading to disorder (adharma) and violence against the 'other'. His second point emphasizes that the Mahābhārata is first of all an inquiry into the nature of the self in relation to the others, as life is fundamentally about a system of relationships—personal, social, political—grounded in an ethical order or dharma.

Then as now, these ideas revolve around the dichotomy between the particular and the universal, debates on dharma and truth, the role of speech (vāni) in the search for truth, the relative notions of fate and freedom, the dilemmas of violence and conflict between right and wrong—as well as between right and right—the necessity of forgiveness (kshama) and reconciliation, the issues of social order and bondage, the paradox of self-interest, pleasure, happiness in relation to those of the 'other' and finally, the search for knowledge of reality.

In essence, Badrinath provides a discourse that bridges the language of experience and transcendence, distinguishing it from both historical narratives and abstract concepts. This approach offers a unique perspective on tradition, differing from those who view the Mahābhārata solely as itihāsa.

‘This is Kurukshetra, Son.
This is where our kings seek
to die
[. . .]
for a skyway,
swift and direct to heaven.
[. . .]
with lives so slaked, heaven
their only conquest left.

But this is Kurukshetra,
this is where things could
change, Son. I heard the sages
swear: equal will all men be, in hell
or heaven, once killed here. Think, if
even the pariahs – Mahar and Shanar,
Chamar and Chandal, Dhobi, Bhangi,
[. . .]
can attain
casteless paradise.'[18]

In another illustration of how the mythical world can be read and reread, Karthika Nair's *Until the Lions: Echoes from the Mahābhārata* offers us the voices of kings and warriors, sages and gods, but also of peasants, slaves, parents, children and the forgotten—and most importantly, from her present.

This retelling is prefaced with a quote from Chinua Achebe that lends the book its title: 'Until the lions have their own historians, the history of the hunt will always glorify the hunter.' The writer must dialogue with the past in meaningful ways, highlighting the reality and presence of marginalized voices—the lions—and not the hunter.

Was myth-making easier in the ancient world?

Myths crafted in contemporary times often become more harmful, rigid, and ideologically entrenched. If we use the term myth to describe a certain ideological adherence, these modern myths spread rapidly through social media. However, most myths originate in societies where orality prevails—where speaking and hearing are central to myth-making. This oral tradition continues to hold value in its origin and space, fostering a process of remembering, retelling, and hearing. Contemporary myth-making can rigidly engrave a particular view of oneself or one's group, often masquerading as truth. Yet, myths are not about truth; they offer a way of viewing reality, which changes over historical time. The Itihāsa-Purāṇa tradition is not about factual truth but about capturing different realities through how people remember their past.

The Mahābhārata and Rāmāyaṇa mention numerous places across India—can these be considered archaeological evidence supporting the historical truth of these epics?

The collective historical consciousness blends mythology and history. This consciousness encompasses memories not only of time but also of space and geography. The concept of Jambudvīpa and

Bhāratavarṣa, for instance, is visualized in local contexts, reflecting how these ideas are transported into local narratives. Jambudvīpa was the region where Bhāratavarṣa was located. This concept, though seemingly imaginary, holds significant importance in Indic traditions, as its representation differs greatly from modern historical mapping methods.

During a village-to-village survey conducted by officers of the State Department of Archaeology and Museums, Government of Andhra Pradesh, an engraving depicting this ancient vision of Jambudvīpa was discovered in the remote village of Konakondla, located in the Vajrakarur Mandal of Anantapur District, Andhra Pradesh. The engraving, carved in stone, closely follows the early Brahmanical myth of the universe's origin. However, it appears that this cosmological depiction was carried to the region through the Jaina tradition, as evidenced by several images of Jaina Tīrthaṅkaras carved on granite slabs on nearby boulders.

According to one source, the probable date of this engraving is suggested to be from the early centuries CE.[19] The term Bhāratavarṣa appears in historical records as Bhāradhavasa for the first time in the Hāthīgumphā inscription of Khāravela (first century BCE).[20]

The mention of various places in these epics results from their continuous reading and reinterpretation across different locations. Additionally, textual interpolations complicate this project. The assumption of a single linear text is misleading; instead, we have multiple versions reflecting a collective historical consciousness.

VIEW FROM THE JWALA NARASIṀHA TEMPLE, AHOBILAM

I do not want to abandon the Chenchu myth we began with as a mere ethnographic note, nor do I want to limit the discussion to a lament of their present condition as a marginalized, impoverished community. The Chenchus have a history, and retrieving it involves not only considering their myths but also their connections to the Itihāsa-Purāṇa tradition. The retelling of their myth is tied to a Purāṇa narrative that centres around

Ahobilam in the Nallamala hills of Andhra Pradesh, where nine shrines are dedicated to Viṣṇu's incarnation as Narasiṃha—half-man, half-lion—a ferocious and aggressive avatāra.

Around these nine shrines, local Purāṇas and Mahātmyas developed, drawing upon the story of Hiraṇyakaśipu, Prahlāda and Narasiṁha.

The myth centres on the slaying of the asura (demon) Hiraṇyakaśipu (literally, 'golden-clothed') by Viṣṇu, to protect demon's pious son, Prahlāda. To accomplish this, Viṣṇu takes the form of his avatāra, Narasiṁha, who emerges from a stone pillar in the asura's palace and hence is often depicted as Sthanaka Narasiṁha—an image vividly represented at Ahobilam.

Another common depiction shows him tearing open Hiraṇyakaśipu's belly, with the demon sprawled across Narasiṁha's lap. These dramatic moments, along with other elements of the myth, are intricately carved onto the walls of the nine shrines and their adjacent halls at Ahobilam.

In various Purāṇas, Prahlāda is occasionally shown returning to his asura nature, as he is expected to uphold his asura dharma. However, an important aspect of the myth—emphasized in local traditions—is his unwavering devotion to Narasiṁha, despite being the son of Hiraṇyakaśipu. This theme is powerfully integrated into the local context through artistic representations at these shrines. One particular cavern even houses a

NARASIṀHA APPREHENDS HIRAṆYAKAŚIPU

EMERGING FROM A PILLAR: STHANAKA NARASIṀHA

shrine dedicated to Prahlāda, where he is worshiped as a deity in this regional tradition.

A significant takeaway from this myth is that conflict with the 'Other' can be resolved in two ways: through outright war or through devotion. The transformation of Prahlāda into a devoted follower of Viṣṇu, as visually depicted at Ahobilam, may have served as a reminder to the local population that submission to the divine was ultimately for their own wellbeing.

Interestingly, in some of these shrines, Lord Narasiṃha is depicted as a hunter, leading some to argue that he may have originally been a deity of the forests. However, his iconography consistently portrays him as half-man

PRAHLĀDA VARADA LAKSHMI NARASIṀHA TEMPLE, AHOBILAM

IN HIS CALM STATE: YOGANANDA NARASIṀHA

and half-lion. The temple in upper Ahobilam features Ugra Narasiṃha (the fierce form), while the lower depicts him as Sri Lakṣmī Narasiṃha Swamy, in a calm state.

The Chenchus inhabiting the hills around these shrines were historically categorized into groups such as Adi, Yanadi and Dasari, as noted by Colin Mackenzie in the eighteenth century. These descriptions suggest a diverse community, not entirely subordinated; some may have resisted attempts by

dominant societies to claim their women or integrate them into the prevailing religious sensibilities. One group of Chenchus, according to nineteenth century accounts, even claimed Narasiṃha as their brother-in-law. And some members of this community became part of the narrative depicted in the art of these shrines, creating concrete historical evidence that illustrates Narasiṃha's deep relationship with the Chenchus.

HUNTERS, AHOBILA NARASIṂHA TEMPLE, AHOBILAM

How does myth find its way into the historical record? The myth that began this book was that of Chenchita, who did not wish to be born beautiful because she was taken away by nawabs and the gods. The earliest-known historical record of Chenchita appears in an inscription in the raṅgamaṇḍapa (pavilion) of a Narasiṃha temple built on a hill at Korukonda in the East Godavari district. This inscription states that the temple was built by a

Lakṣmī dāsi in 1354. An image depicts Chenchita standing with a bow in her hand while Narasiṃha holds her leg and removes a thorn from her foot. Similar but smaller images can be found on pillars in the kalyāna maṇḍapa (marriage hall) of the same temple.

There are three or four sculptures from Ahobilam that depict Narasiṃha wooing Chenchita, and one particularly notable example was commissioned by Harihara II of the Vijayanagara dynasty in 1395. In this sculpture, the two stand on a pedestal, with Narasiṃha in a pleading stance. His palm is placed between her neck and breast, while she appears outwardly angry, looking straight ahead. Narasiṃha, with his mouth open, holds her chin, as if trying to appeal to her, but she remains unaffected by his efforts. She is shown holding a bow and arrow in her left hand. This sculpture evokes local myths and legends that speak of the anger of Chenchita at being carried away by the god.

A similar sculpture with the same posture has been found on a pillar in the Ugra Narasiṃhaswamy temple at Peddamudlyam in the Cuddapah district, although the face of Chenchita in this depiction has suffered damage. The sculptors of these medieval temples skilfully captured the emotional valence of these narratives. In other locations, such as the kalyāna maṇḍapams, standalone images of Chenchu Lakṣmī are also found. These portray her with a bow and arrow, either hunting or joyfully enacting her traditional roles. The dynamic postures on the pillars and walls at Ahobilam suggest that this motif became popular, integrating the Chenchus into the artistic and cultural expressions of the period.

There were periods of crisis—such as when the temple was attacked by Turkish invaders from the north. This occurred in 1619 during the reign of King Ramadevaraya, as recorded in the Ahobilam kaifiyats (village histories). Incursions by Muslim invaders had begun earlier, during the reign of King Rangarayadeva (1578–87), prompting local pontiffs to appeal for the temple's restoration to its original glory. In the sixteenth century, the seventh pontiff of the Ahobilam Math, Vamsatha Gopa Jiyyamgar, wrote the Sanksrit play

WORSHIPPERS FROM THE PLAINS, LAKṢMĪ NARASIṀHA TEMPLE, AHOBILAM

Vasantika Parinayam. It centres on the marriage of Lord Narasiṃha with a Chenchu woman from the Nallamala forests. While lamenting the state of the present moment, the pontiff invokes stories from the past to inspire and energize local devotees and encourage them to return to the temple. This effort also appealed to Vijayanagara kings for continued material support for the shrine.

But who were these devotees surrounding the temple? They were the Chenchus, of course, who needed to be reminded of their historical ties to the temple and reengaged during a period of crisis. The play metaphorically emphasizes dialogue as a means to stabilize human relationships and renew devotion.

The Purāṇic sensibilities and stories surrounding the Narasiṃha–Hiraṇyakaṣipu–Prahlāda narrative were adapted to the local context, resulting in unique regional interpretations. Locally, it is believed that after killing Hiraṇyakaṣipu, Lord Narasiṃha forgot to return to his celestial abode and also forgot about his bride, Lakṣmī. She, however, chose to stay back and was reborn as the daughter of a Chenchu chief. It took some time for

Narasiṃha to meet her again, after which they were married. In this narrative, the Chenchu girl is identified as Lakṣmī herself—a clear attempt by religious orthodoxy to legitimize the Chenchus' presence in the region's folklore. However, the depictions of her anger suggest that the incorporation of the Chenchus into dominant religious ideology was likely not a smooth process.

This tension is evident in an eighth-century poem by the Āḻvār saint Thirumangai, who refers to Ahobilam as Singavelkunram. While praising the site's glories, he warns that 'the twang of bows of the local hunters waylay the pilgrims to the shrine.'

A HUNTER, LAKṢMĪ NARASIṀHA TEMPLE, AHOBILAM

Not all Chenchus, then, were fully integrated into this religious narrative and they may have posed a significant threat to non-tribal populations in surrounding areas. Many Chenchus remained outside this discourse, indicating that their incorporation was fraught with contestation and danger.

These complex conjunctures of negotiations transformed the myth within its local context. Social interactions between communities led to both the myth and Chenchu sentiments being historicized into tangible representations that have survived over time. Thus, memory and history both play a role in how the past is perceived. While the Chenchus do not deny their close relationship with Narasiṃha, they interpret it differently. From their perspective, the women of their community were at risk of being taken by dominant groups, highlighting a gendered dimension to this interaction that must not be overlooked. Perhaps, Chenchu Lakṣmī's incorporation into the pantheon served to address this injustice while granting the Chenchus certain ritual privileges at temple sites.

In a regional context, the Hiraṇyakaṣipu–Prahlāda myth was creatively adapted to a forested locality, serving as a medium that connected it to a larger civilizational framework while maintaining its distinctiveness. However, as is typical of Purāṇic stories, there is no definitive conclusion. The narrative remains open-ended and ambiguous, allowing for continual reinterpretation. On a deeper level, such storytelling aims to explore the relationship between the 'self' and the 'other'. These narratives do not offer conclusive messages but instead encourage reflection—of oneself as an individual, as part of society or a region—and interrogation of why or why not these stories remain relevant.

Thus, a study of time and history in the Purāṇas reveals how elite identities were resurrected through specific interpretations of the past—blending cyclic frameworks like manvantaras and yugas with emerging linearity. Even as these ideas dispersed regionally, they reinforced elite power by shaping the construction of dynastic and ruler identities. While reckoning with the 'other' in exclusionary ways, these narratives also attempted to reconcile power dynamics and its distribution.

But these texts are not merely about the past. Badrinath's exploration of the Mahābhārata emphasized how time was viewed as both linear (in the short term) and cyclic (philosophically), embroiled in ethical dilemmas. His work underscores that these questions of identity are not relics of the past but resonate in every contemporary era, each grappling uniquely with the human condition.

The underlying tension in these processes is undeniable. Yet, the multiplicity of how the past was remembered and visually embedded into history tells a powerful story—not merely one of imposition but one where fragments of the subaltern's experiences also got through. These interactions are usually renewed annually through ritual re-enactments, transforming myth from a distant past into a living present for local communities.

The Itihāsa-Purāṇa tradition sustains a continual dialogue between myth and history, preserving distinct identities rather than merging them into a monolithic narrative sanctioned by modern historiography. Modern historians must now ask: Are memory and visual representation viable tools for recovering the past, beyond written or inscribed words?

The conundrum of the present lies in the use of history to rectify past wrongs—an approach foreign to the Itihāsa-Purāṇa tradition, which remembers the past through the lens of present relevance, emphasizing ethical essence over factual verification. History, on the other hand, as the handmaiden of the modern nation-state often seeks to 'prove' past injustices or legitimize state power, manipulating societal sentiments tied to emotional experiences of the past.

One thing is certain: We must move away from a positivist use of mythology, where the 'truth' of a myth is misused as a valid source for historical events. Modern historiography has evolved far beyond its conventional role of chronicling political events or seeking rational causality.

Are we looking for the truth? Most historians recognize this as unattainable. Instead, we bring the past into the present, transforming it into a contested terrain for current struggles. Historical reality, if paintable at all, must emerge from our myriad identities—yielding multiple, coexisting truths. Inclusivity in history demands that our inquiry into myth and history take a new turn: one that embraces ambiguity, centres marginalized voices and acknowledges that the past, like the present, is a mosaic of perspectives.

NOTES

1 Christoph von Fürer-Haimendorf, 'Why Chenchu Women Are Not Beautiful' in *The Chenchus: Jungle Folk of the Deccan*, The Aboriginal Tribes of Hyderabad, VOL. 1 (Macmillan, 1943), p. 227.

2 Edgar Thurston, 'Chenchu' in *Castes and Tribes of Southern India*, VOL. 2 (Government Press, 1909), p. 27.

3 Thurston, 'Chenchu', p. 42.

4 Thurston, 'Chenchu', p. 42.

5 Ashis Nandy, 'History's Forgotten Doubles', History and Theory 34(2) (1995): 44.

6 Nandy, 'History's Forgotten Doubles': 44.

7 Dipesh Chakrabarty, 'Postcoloniality and the Artifice of History: Who Speaks for "Indian" Pasts?', *Representations* 37 (Winter 1992): 1–26; here, p. 18.

8 L. P. Vidyarthi, 'Folklore Research in India' in Alan Dundes (ed.), *Varia Folklorica* (De Gruyter Mouton, 1978), pp. 201–62. See also D. N. Bhagvat, *An Outline of Indian Folklore* (Popular Book Depot, 1958).

9 Bernard Lewis, *History: Remembered, Recovered, Invented* (Simon & Schuster, 1987), p. 12.

10 Romila Thapar, *The Past Before Us: Historical Traditions of Early North India* (Permanent Black, 2013), p. 275.

11 Thapar, *Past Before Us*, p. 276.

12 Thapar, *Past Before Us*, p. 280.

13 Thapar, *Past Before Us*, p. 308.

14 Aruna Pariti, *Genealogy, Time and Identity: Historical Consciousness in the Deccan, Sixth Century* CE*–Twelfth Century* CE (Primus Books, 2015).

15 Pariti, *Genealogy, Time and Identity*, pp. 76–77.

16 Chaturvedi Badrinath, *The Mahābhārata: An Inquiry in the Human Condition* (Hyderabad: Orient Longman, 2006), p. 4.

17 Badrinath, *Mahābhārata*, p. 9.

18 Karthika Nair, 'Pawn Talk: Brass and String' in *Until the Lions: Echoes from the Mahābhārata* (HarperCollins, 2015).

19 K. Rama Mohan Rao and B. Subrahmanyan (eds), *The Directory of Monuments and Antiquarian Remains of Andhra Pradesh*, VOL. 1 (Anantapur District, PART I), Archaeological Series 70 (Government of Andhra Pradesh, 1993), pp. 310–12.

20 K. P. Jayaswal, 'The Hāthīgumphā Inscription of Khāravela', *Epigraphica Indica* 20 (1912): 79.